REBEL ALLIANCE

INTRODUCTION

The heroic Rebel Alliance fights for freedom across the LEGO® *Star Wars* galaxy. From the dashing Han Solo to the timid C-3PO, learn all about this rag-tag force of brave minifigures.

HOW TO USE THIS BOOK

These amazing minifigures are ordered according to the *Star Wars*® property in which they first appeared or mostly featured. Tabs at the top of each page indicate which properties this minifgure appears in. As most Star Wars characters appear in the Expanded Universe, that tab is highlighted only if a minifigure appears in an EU set. The Clone Wars tab has not been highlighted if the character has a separate Clone Wars minifigure.

This book also includes variants of featured minifigures, which are the same character, but have some modifications that make them different in some way.

Introduction
MEET THE MINIFIGURES

Contents

Brave astromech droid R2-D2 has ventured into 22 LEGO *Star Wars* sets to date, making him the most recurring minifigure in the LEGO line. R2-D2's head was redesigned in 2008, but the rest of him has remained the same since his release in 1999, with one exception: In Jabba's Sail Barge (set 6210), poor R2 is forced to carry drinks on a serving tray.

Jedi Starfighter (set 7256)

R2-D2's head piece alone appears in two sets: Jedi Starfighter (set 7256) and Ultimate Space Battle (set 7283). Only R2-D2's head is visible when he is in flight mode, navigating his owner safely through space aboard a Jedi Starfighter.

STAR VARIANT

Jabba's droid

R2-D2 is set to work serving Jabba the Hutt and his low-life friends in the 2006 set Jabba's Sail Barge (set 6210). He has a serving tray with drinks between his head and body pieces.

R2-D2
ASTROMECH DROID

Holoprojector transmits holographic images and acts as a spotlight

Camera eye records messages

LEGO R2-D2 had a white head with silver and blue printing before his redesign in 2008, when he acquired this bluish-gray head

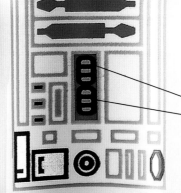

DATA FILE

SET: 7877 Naboo Starfighter
YEAR: 2011
PIECES: 4
EQUIPMENT: None
VARIANTS: 3

LEGO Technic pins join R2-D2's legs to his body

Acoustic signaler and ventilation point

Astromech

When R2-D2 was first released in 1999, his entire body was made from unique LEGO pieces. Since then, all LEGO *Star Wars* astromech droids have used the same pieces but with varying printing and colors.

STAR VARIANTS

Chrome gold
This limited edition chrome gold C-3PO was randomly placed in 10,000 LEGO *Star Wars* sets to celebrate the 30th anniversary of *Star Wars* in 2007. The LEGO Group also made five 14-carat gold variants.

Light C-3PO
The original variant of C-3PO is light pearl-gold in color. It appeared in sets between 2001 and 2005. From 2008, the color of C-3PO changed to a richer pearl-gold.

Worrisome protocol droid

C-3PO has found himself in ten LEGO *Star Wars* sets since he was first released in 2001. C-3PO was the first LEGO *Star Wars* protocol droid and seven variants of him have since been released. All have kept his original protocol head-mold and printing but his gold tone has been refined from light pearl-gold to a brighter pearl-gold color.

Audiosensor—C-3PO has one on each side of his head

C-3PO's connection wires are exposed in his mid-body section

Behind C-3PO
C-3PO's shiny gold armor continues on the back of his torso piece. You can also see his back plate and mid-body section.

Protocol droids
C-3PO was the first LEGO protocol droid and his head-mold was specially cast for him. The LEGO Group has since produced other protocol droids using the same head-mold: R-3PO, K-3PO (pp.19–20), and the Death Star Droid.

DATA FILE
SET: 8092 Luke's Landspeeder
YEAR: 2010
PIECES: 3
EQUIPMENT: None
VARIANTS: 7

Plain pearl gold hips and legs are unique to C-3PO

C-3PO PROTOCOL DROID

7

This cool-headed captain of the consular cruiser *Tantive IV* is on a covert mission for the Rebel Alliance—he must transport secret Death Star plans across the galaxy. When his ship is invaded by Darth Vader, brave Antilles refuses to betray the location of the plans. However, swiveling the minifigure's double-sided head reveals the fate of his own personal mission!

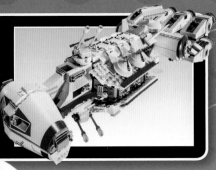

Tantive IV (set 10198)
Captain Raymus Antilles is exclusive to this 2009 set. He commands the *Tantive IV* from a central control room which has two monitors for the minifigure to track the ship's progress on.

LEGO Death
Captain Antilles meets a grizzly end when Darth Vader strangles him! This face shows his pained expression.

Captain Antilles
ILL-FATED CAPTAIN

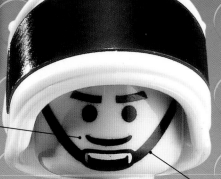

Captain Antilles happily goes about his work for the Rebel Alliance

Rank badge with five blue dots shows this minifigure is a captain

Helmet strap with white chin guard is printed on Captain Antilles's face

Torso with open utility jacket and gray undershirt is unique to this minifigure. The dark-tan shoulder panels of Captain Antilles's jacket continue on the back of his torso

DATA FILE
SET: 10198 *Tantive IV*
YEAR: 2009
PIECES: 5
EQUIPMENT: None
VARIANTS: 1

Rebel Scout Speeder (7668)

This 2008 set was the first to contain the Rebel trooper minifigure—with enough to start a Rebel Army! Four Rebel troopers fit into the repulsorlift speeder: a pilot, two soldiers, and a gunner atop the turret.

This Rebel trooper is ready to fight for the Alliance! His minifigure comes well equipped for battle in his custom-made blast helmet, wielding plenty of fire power. The Rebel trooper has starred in just two sets—he arrived with several comrades in the first, and provides vital backup for Captain Antilles in the second.

Removeable blast visor clips into holes at the sides of the helmet

Only the Rebel trooper and Captain Antilles (opposite) wear this blast helmet

Rebel helmet

This white blast helmet with an extended neck guard was specially designed for this minifigure.

Rebel troopers carry blaster guns like this as well as long blaster rifles

Although the Rebel trooper wears the standard-issue Rebel Army uniform of a sand-blue shirt and black combat vest, the torso is seen only on this minifigure

Rebel Trooper
SOLDIER OF THE REBEL ARMY

DATA FILE

SET: 10198 *Tantive IV*
YEAR: 2009
PIECES: 5
EQUIPMENT: Blaster, blaster rifle
VARIANTS: 1

As a member of the Galactic Senate and secret sympathizer of the Rebel Alliance, Princess Leia Organa is a symbol of hope across the LEGO *Star Wars* galaxy.
She dresses in the traditional white robes of the Alderaan royal family. Her redesigned minifigure, with a double-sided head, escapes the clutches of Darth Vader in the 2011 *Millennium Falcon* (set 7965).

Princess Leia
SENATOR OF ALDERAAN

Princess Leia wears her hair in two braided buns when on senatorial duty. The LEGO hair piece was specially created for Leia's minifigure

STAR VARIANT

Original Leia
The first variant of Princess Leia appears in the original *Millennium Falcon* (set 7190), released in 2000. The minifigure has a yellow head and hands, and a unique torso with light gray printing.

Unique LEGO head is first seen on the 2011 design. It has feminine fluttering eyelashes and red lips

Leia wears this white torso piece with black and light bluish-gray printing in LEGO sets from 2007 onwards

Leia probably stole this blaster from Imperial forces!

Serious side
While one side of Princess Leia's face has a relaxed smile, the other has a determined expression.

Symbolic silver belt of Alderaan royalty

DATA FILE
SET: 7965 *Millennium Falcon*
YEAR: 2011
PIECES: 4
EQUIPMENT: Blaster
VARIANTS: 4

STAR VARIANT

First Luke
The original variant of young Luke Skywalker has short tan hair, a yellow face and hands, and different printing on his torso and leg pieces. He appears in three 2000–2003 LEGO sets.

Luke wore standard long female LEGO hair from 2007 until this unique hair was created for his 2011 redesign

Luke Skywalker is a poor farmboy who dreams of becoming a space pilot. The sullen expression on one side of his minifigure's dual-face head shows just how much he longs to escape the daily drudgery of life on his uncle's moisture farm! But when Luke meets exiled Jedi Obi-Wan Kenobi, his life changes forever.

Unique head with a down-turned mouth and distinctive chin dimple is new for the 2011 redesign

Helmet head
Luke wears a helmet with a visor as a blindfold when he practices using the Force with his lightsaber.

Obi-Wan Kenobi gave Luke this blue lightsaber

Luke keeps farm tools in his brown utility belt pouch

Luke Skywalker
FARMBOY OF TATOOINE

DATA FILE
SET: 7965 *Millennium Falcon*
YEAR: 2011
PIECES: 4
EQUIPMENT: Blaster, lightsaber
VARIANTS: 4

Leg bindings keep out desert sand

Obi-Wan "Ben" Kenobi
EXILED JEDI

Now an old man, Obi-Wan Kenobi is a Jedi in exile. He lives a hermit's existence on Tatooine and goes by the name of Ben Kenobi. But his minifigure shows signs of the life he once led: He wears Jedi robes and a brown cloak, and keeps his blue lightsaber close at hand. Obi-Wan "Ben" Kenobi appears in six LEGO *Star Wars* sets.

Luke's Landspeeder (set 8092)

Obi-Wan Kenobi accompanies Luke Skywalker in his landspeeder in this 2010 set. It has a secret compartment to hold the minifigures' lightsabers.

Obi-Wan Kenobi is a Jedi in exile, but he still has his blue lightsaber

Old Obi-Wan has a gray beard and wrinkles. The minifigure has had this LEGO head since 2010

Only old Obi-Wan Kenobi wears these tan robes and simple brown belt. In sets released before 2007, he has a torso with fewer robe details and no belt

DATA FILE

SET: 7965 *Millennium Falcon*
YEAR: 2011
PIECES: 5
EQUIPMENT: Cape, lightsaber
VARIANTS: 6

STAR VARIANT

Original Obi
This variant of old Obi-Wan Kenobi appears in the Landspeeder (set 7110). He has a yellow head and hands, simple torso printing, brown hips, and no hood or cape.

STAR VARIANT

Original Wookiee

The first Chewbacca minifigure is made from the same pieces as the later variant, but they are all colored brown instead of reddish-brown. The minifigure appears in three 2000–2001 sets.

The head and textured body are made from a single sandwich-board piece that fits over a standard reddish-brown minifigure torso

Wookiee Chewbacca is a brave fighter and long-time companion of Han Solo. Although Chewie towers over his friend in the *Star Wars* movies, his LEGO minifigure is average height. Chewbacca appears in 11 LEGO sets, never hesitating to protect his home planet of Kashyyyk from Separatist invasion or fight alongside the Rebels.

Molded to give hairy texture

DATA FILE

SET: 7879 Hoth Echo Base
YEAR: 2011
PIECES: 3
EQUIPMENT: Bowcaster
VARIANTS: 2

Bandolier contains energy bolts for the Wookiee bowcaster

Comic-Con exclusive

In 2009, a handcuffed brown Chewbacca minifigure appeared in a collectible display set made exclusively for San Diego's Comic-Con, with Luke Skywalker and Han Solo minifigures in stormtrooper disguise.

LEGO crossbow piece adapted to the distinctive Wookiee bowcaster

Reddish-brown pieces replace the original brown ones

Chewbacca
WOOKIEE HERO

13

This bold minifigure is a loveable LEGO *Star Wars* rogue! The unlikely hero who found himself mixed up in the Rebellion against the Empire has starred in eight LEGO *Star Wars* sets. Like his beaten-up ship, the *Millennium Falcon*, Han's minifigure has been modified over the years—but he has retained his confident smile!

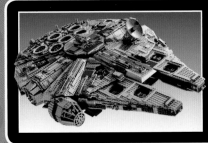

Millennium Falcon (set 10179)

This 2007 version of Han's battered YT-1300 light freighter, the *Millennium Falcon*, is an Ultimate Collector's Edition set. The cockpit seats four minifigures, with Han and his right-hand Wookiee Chewbacca at the helm!

STAR VARIANT

Solo Solo
This is a rare original variant of Han Solo's minifigure. He appears in only one LEGO set: the first-ever LEGO *Millennium Falcon* (set 7190), released in 2000.

Harrison Ford
Han Solo is the first LEGO minifigure to be based on the likeness of actor Harrison Ford, who plays Han Solo in the *Star Wars* movies—but he is not the only one to be based on Ford! There is also a LEGO Indiana Jones.

Han Solo
BRAVE BRAGGART

Han wears a black vest and light shirt

This light flesh head with white pupils is first seen in the 2011 design

Unique painted hips feature pockets for Han's essentials, including a droid caller and blaster power cell reserves

Previous variants of this minifigure have featured brown and blue legs, but Han is hardly ever without his gun belt and quick-draw holster

DATA FILE

SET: 7965 *Millennium Falcon*
YEAR: 2011
PIECES: 4
EQUIPMENT: Blaster
VARIANTS: 5

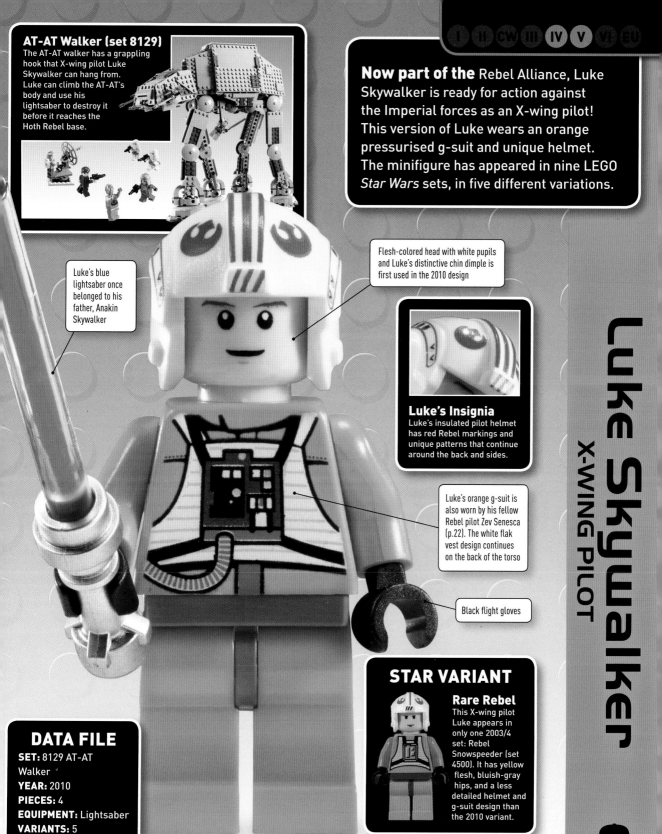

AT-AT Walker (set 8129)
The AT-AT walker has a grappling hook that X-wing pilot Luke Skywalker can hang from. Luke can climb the AT-AT's body and use his lightsaber to destroy it before it reaches the Hoth Rebel base.

Now part of the Rebel Alliance, Luke Skywalker is ready for action against the Imperial forces as an X-wing pilot! This version of Luke wears an orange pressurised g-suit and unique helmet. The minifigure has appeared in nine LEGO *Star Wars* sets, in five different variations.

Flesh-colored head with white pupils and Luke's distinctive chin dimple is first used in the 2010 design

Luke's blue lightsaber once belonged to his father, Anakin Skywalker

Luke's Insignia
Luke's insulated pilot helmet has red Rebel markings and unique patterns that continue around the back and sides.

Luke's orange g-suit is also worn by his fellow Rebel pilot Zev Senesca (p.22). The white flak vest design continues on the back of the torso

Black flight gloves

Luke Skywalker
X-WING PILOT

STAR VARIANT
Rare Rebel
This X-wing pilot Luke appears in only one 2003/4 set: Rebel Snowspeeder (set 4500). It has yellow flesh, bluish-gray hips, and a less detailed helmet and g-suit design than the 2010 variant.

DATA FILE
SET: 8129 AT-AT Walker
YEAR: 2010
PIECES: 4
EQUIPMENT: Lightsaber
VARIANTS: 5

15

Ace X-wing pilot Wedge Antilles is the hero of three huge battles—Yavin, Hoth, and Endor—but he has featured in only one LEGO *Star Wars* set. Humble hero Wedge blends in among the other X-wing pilot minifigures in his Rebel flight suit and standard minifigure face, but his unique helmet sets him apart from the rest.

Wedge Antilles
X-WING PILOT

X-Wing Fighter (set 6212)
Wedge Antilles is exclusive to the 2006 X-Wing Fighter set, which also includes X-wing pilot Luke Skywalker (p.15). The vehicle can change from Luke's Red Five to Wedge's Red Two X-wing with its unique wing details.

This simple, smiling face appears on 14 LEGO minifigures, including LEGO *Star Wars* pilots Dutch Vander (p.18) and Dak Ralter (p.23)

The same torso pattern is used—but on a red torso—for the B-wing pilot minifigure

This orange pressurized g-suit is standard issue flight wear for LEGO X-wing pilots. It protects them from dangerous acceleration g-forces when flying at high speeds

DATA FILE
SET: 6212 X-Wing Fighter
YEAR: 2006
PIECES: 4
EQUIPMENT: None
VARIANTS: 1

Black flight gloves

Custom helmet
Wedge's custom-made X-wing pilot helmet has dark bluish-gray rectangles and a circle pattern along the sides.

X-Wing Fighter (set 7140)
This X-Wing Fighter LEGO set includes two X-wing pilots—Biggs and his fellow Red Squadron pilot Luke Skywalker. The starship's cockpit does not have room for both pilots to fly together, so while one pilot takes flight, the other can wait on the ground with the fully equipped Rebel Technician minifigure.

Custom helmet with chequered pattern and Rebel insignia

Brave X-wing pilot Biggs Darklighter appears with his childhood friend Luke Skywalker in the X-Wing Fighter (set 7140). He has remained exclusive to the set since its release in 1999. Known to his fellow Rebel pilots as "Red Three," Biggs's insulated flying helmet has a unique pattern on it. Biggs was killed in the Rebel's assault on the first Death Star.

Yellow heads were used on LEGO *Star Wars* minifigures from 1999 to 2004

The printing on this early X-wing pilot torso piece has fewer details than that worn by Luke Skywalker (p.15)

Chest pack straps

Biggs Darklighter
X-WING PILOT

Mustache man
Biggs's mustachioed head is only used on his minifigure in the LEGO *Star Wars* theme, but it is used in lots of other LEGO themes for characters such as waiters, chefs, coast guards, and firemen.

DATA FILE
SET: 7140 X-Wing Fighter
YEAR: 1999
PIECES: 4
EQUIPMENT: None
VARIANTS: 1

Daring Jon "Dutch" Vander has the call-sign Gold Leader when he flies into battle as a Rebel pilot, but he is shot down in the Battle of Yavin. He is one of the only minifigures to have ever flown a LEGO Y-wing fighter. He appears in the starships in three LEGO *Star Wars* sets (and in two re-releases).

Dutch wears a unique helmet with a yellow grid pattern and Rebel insignia

STAR VARIANT

Yellow Dutch
This Dutch Vander variant has a yellow head with red hair and eyebrows and a headset to help him communicate with his squadron. It appears in the 1999 set TIE Fighter and Y-Wing (set 7150) and its 2002 and 2004 re-releases.

DATA FILE
SET: 7658 Y-Wing Fighter
YEAR: 2007
PIECES: 4
EQUIPMENT: Blaster
VARIANTS: 3

X- and Y-wing pilots wear these life support units to help them breathe during flight

Dutch Vander
Y-WING PILOT

Dutch is one of the only Rebel pilots to carry a blaster

This Dutch has blue-gray hips, but an early variant has dark gray hips

Hoth Rebel Base (set 7666)
K-3PO has only ever appeared in this limited edition 2007 set, making him a rare LEGO minifigure. K-3PO watches from the sliding doors of the command center as Hoth Rebel trooper minifigures face off with Imperial snowtroopers who are attacking the Rebel base.

K-3PO is a one-of-a-kind droid in more ways than one. The white protocol droid is an invaluable tactical expert in the Rebel army—so much so that the Alliance High Command awarded him the position of lieutenant. He is also a limited-edition LEGO *Star Wars* minifigure that is exclusive to one set: Hoth Rebel Base (set 7666), released in 2007.

K-3PO is branded with two red dots that identify him as a Rebel lieutenant

K-3PO has the same head-mold as fellow protocol droids C-3PO (p.7), R-3PO (p.20), and the Death Star droid, but only he has it in white

Protocol print
Although K-3PO has special rank branding on his torso piece, the rest of his printing is the same as that seen on other protocol droid minifigures. Their back armor details are also identical.

Ridged pelvic armor plate

K-3PO's entire form is covered with white armor. He would feel naked without it!

DATA FILE
SET: 7666 Hoth Rebel Base
YEAR: 2011
PIECES: 3
EQUIPMENT: None
VARIANTS: 1

K-3PO
REBEL LIEUTENANT

With his bright red coloring and
a markedly moody disposition,
R-3PO might not seem like the best
choice for a spy droid detector at
Hoth Echo Base (set 7879), but
that's exactly why he is one! No one
suspects a thing, and this inquisitive
minifigure has foiled many Imperial
infiltration attempts on Hoth.
R-3PO makes his first appearance
in LEGO *Star Wars* in 2011.

Hoth Echo Base (set 7879)

R-3PO serves under the
Rebel Alliance at their
secret base on Hoth.
He is known for having a
very moody disposition, and
proves to be a general
annoyance around the
place. His minifigure first
appears in this 2011 set.

R-3PO performs his
espionage duties by
closely observing
others with his
photoreceptors

R-3PO cuts a
conspicuous figure
in his red protocol
droid armor

Although R-3PO is
a droid, he has a
human-like build, so
his minifigure has
standard arm, hand,
torso, and leg pieces

Printed plate
pattern continues
on the back of
R-3PO's torso

R-3PO
REBEL ESPIONAGE DROID

DATA FILE
SET: 7879 Hoth Echo
Base
YEAR: 2011
PIECES: 3
EQUIPMENT: None
VARIANTS: 1

No tattoo
R-3PO is thought to sport
a tattoo on his left
posterior that says "Thank
the Maker," but there is no
sign of it on his LEGO
minifigure! R-3PO has
plain red minifigure hip
and leg pieces.

Hoth Helmets

These variants of the Hoth Rebel trooper minifigure wear different Hoth head gear. Each has a white aviator helmet, and one has a brown visor, one has rounded white snow goggles, and another has new-style snow goggles.

The secret Rebel headquarters are now on the hostile ice planet Hoth, so the Rebel trooper minifigure wears an insulated uniform and helmet. He appears in six sets, each containing a different variant—but all six are dressed to battle both the cold weather and the Empire!

This tan insulated helmet is first seen on the 2010 design. Luke Skywalker in his Hoth gear also wears the helmet

Backpack is attached around the minifigure's neck. All six variants of the Hoth Rebel trooper wear this piece

Backpack
Only the Hoth Rebel trooper minifigure wears this white backpack with a bedroll in LEGO *Star Wars*.

Unique torso design with a white scarf, tan utility belt, and thermal jacket is first seen in 2010

DL-21 blaster with targeting scope

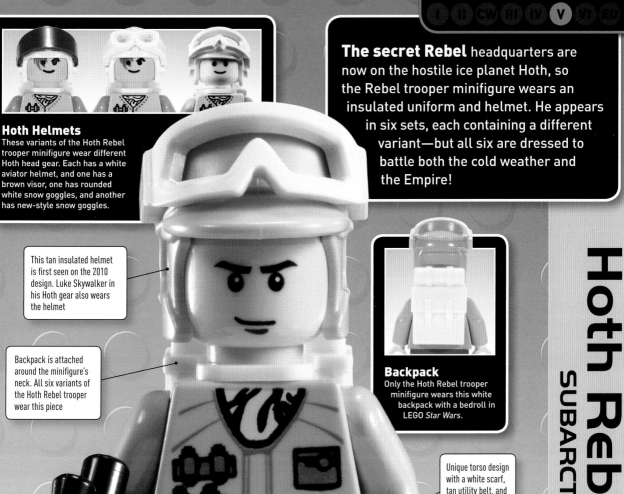

Hoth Rebel Trooper
SUBARCTIC SOLDIER

DATA FILE

SET: 8129 AT-AT Walker
YEAR: 2010
PIECES: 6
EQUIPMENT: Blaster
VARIANTS: 6

21

Zev Senesca is a brave Rebel X-wing pilot who fights on Hoth. He is the only X-wing pilot to carry a weapon, making him especially effective during combat. His minifigure appears in two sets and is a pioneer in its design. Zev's 2009 head and torso have since appeared elsewhere in the LEGO *Star Wars* galaxy.

Each X-wing pilot wears a unique helmet. Zev's has distinctive gray markings

All in a name
Zev Senesca was the first named character to feature in a LEGO *Star Wars* battle pack. Previously, the minifigures included in the LEGO battle packs were generic troopers and pilots.

Zev's head is printed with an orange visor and chin strap. It is also seen on the Clone pilot and Captain Jag minifigures

Zev Senesca
X-WING PILOT

Zev does not rely on his X-wing's fire power alone—he also keeps a blaster close at hand during flight

Zev's flight suit torso features a white flak vest and detailed life-support chest pack

Back detail
Zev was the first LEGO X-wing pilot to feature a double-sided torso. X-wing pilot Luke Skywalker (p.15) adopted the torso piece later in 2010.

Standard-issue orange pressurized jumpsuit

DATA FILE

SET: 8089 Hoth Wampa Cave
YEAR: 2010
PIECES: 4
EQUIPMENT: Blaster
VARIANTS: 1

STAR VARIANT

Yellow head

Dak Ralter has yellow flesh and darker gray hips in the 1999 Snowspeeder (set 7130). Another variant in the 2003 Rebel Snowspeeder (set 4500) also has yellow flesh, but he has the same light bluish-gray hips as seen on the 2007 variant.

There are two blue Rebel Alliance symbols on Dak's unique helmet

Doomed Rebel pilot Dak Ralter is a gunner in Luke Skywalker's snowspeeder on Hoth. His happy and naive expression belies a murky fate. Dak looks a lot like other X-wing pilot minifigures but his helmet makes him unique. Dak has appeared in three LEGO sets.

Visor visibility

X-wing pilots' helmets often have an orange visor that contains a special computer screen to help them with targeting during battle. However, Dak's minifigure does not have one—he must think he doesn't need it!

Dak's torso piece is also worn by his fellow Rebel pilots Luke Skywalker, Biggs Darklighter, Wedge Antilles (p. 16), and Dutch Vander (p.18)

Dak wears standard issue X-wing pilot black flight gloves

Dak Ralter
X-WING PILOT

Bending Dak's poseable legs at his hip joint allows the minifigure to fit in the snowspeeder cockpit alongside his co-pilot, Luke Skywalker

DATA FILE

SET: 7666 Hoth Rebel Base
YEAR: 2007
PIECES: 4
EQUIPMENT: None
VARIANTS: 3

This cool customer is the Baron Administrator of Cloud City. Lando Calrissian has a flamboyant personality and sense of style—something that is reflected in his LEGO minifigure, with his extravagant yellow-lined cloak and baronial outfit. Lando in all his finery only stars in the 2003 set Cloud City (set 10123), alongside his old gambling partner Han Solo.

Lando's head
This Lando Calrissian has a unique brown head with a suave slim mustache and winning smile! The two other versions of LEGO Lando have the same head piece in a reddish-brown color.

DATA FILE
SET: 10123 Cloud City
YEAR: 2003
PIECES: 5
EQUIPMENT: Blaster, cape
VARIANTS: 1

Lando Calrissian
BARON OF CLOUD CITY

The version of Lando dressed in his General outfit has this same short black hair piece

Unique torso features a dark-blue collared shirt and matching Baron Administrator state belt

Lando's exclusive cape is blue on the outside and yellow on the inside. It is a status symbol that distinguishes him as Baron Administrator of Cloud City

Blaster is made from a LEGO loudhailer piece

STAR VARIANT

Uncreased

The original variant of this minifigure has yellow skin, light eyebrows, and no creases on his shirt—even though it appears in Desert Skiff (set 7104), when Han has just escaped after a few days in a cramped carbonite prison.

This face printing was first seen in 2010 and is used only for Han Solo

Han Solo has been captured by Darth Vader! Dressed in casual brown pants and a plain white shirt, Han's minifigure is frozen inside a block of carbonite and delivered to Jabba the Hutt. His minifigure is so unprepared for his imminent capture that he is even without his trusty blaster!

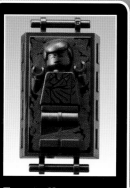

Trapped!

Han is frozen in a block of carbonite! This unique piece cleverly traps Han's minifigure by securing him with clips inside the 3D mold.

Ford's hair

The reddish-brown variant of this common LEGO hair piece is used only for Han Solo in the LEGO *Star Wars* theme. The same color is also used for Indiana Jones's minifigure, which is based on a character also played by actor Harrison Ford.

Detailed printing on Han's unique torso gives his shirt some creases

Han Solo
FROZEN IN CARBONITE

DATA FILE

SET: 8097 *Slave I*
YEAR: 2010
PIECES: 4
EQUIPMENT: None
VARIANTS: 3

Apart from his stormtrooper disguise, this is the only Han Solo minifigure without a gun holster printed on his pants. Han won't be needing a gun where he is going!

Demure Princess Leia is now a scantily clad slave girl—property of Jabba the Hutt! Leia's minifigure is dressed in a gold and dark red slave outfit for the entertainment of the grotesque gangster, with a chain around her neck to keep her in her place. But Jabba better watch out for that chain—Leia might just manage to wrap it around his neck!

Only Leia wears this reddish-brown ponytail piece in LEGO *Star Wars*

Jabba's Sail Barge (set 6210)

Princess Leia is at the mercy of Jabba the Hutt on his sail barge. The enormous crime lord attaches a neck brace and chain to Leia's minifigure to keep his slave close by at all times.

STAR VARIANT

Yellow slave

A variant of Leia in her slave bikini appears in Jabba's Palace (set 4480), released in 2003. She has yellow flesh and brown hair, but the same face and slave outfit pattern.

All versions and variants of Princess Leia in LEGO sets released before 2011 have this same face, with red lips and dainty eyebrows

Princess Leia
JABBA'S SLAVE

Jabba the Hutt forces Leia to wear this revealing gold slave-girl harness

Leia's unique hips and legs are printed with a dark red silk skirt and gold harness briefs

DATA FILE

SET: 6210 Jabba's Sail Barge
YEAR: 2006
PIECES: 4
EQUIPMENT: None
VARIANTS: 2

Home One Mon Calamari Star Cruiser (set 7754)
On board Rebel ship *Home One*, Mon Mothma briefs the other Rebel leaders about plans for the attack on the second Death Star. They gather in the command center around an orange hologram of the Death Star.

Former Senator Mon Mothma is the Supreme Commander of the Rebel Alliance. In her all-white outfit and rare white LEGO cape, her minifigure commands respect from all the Rebel leaders. Mon Mothma is exclusive to the LEGO *Star Wars* set *Home One* Mon Calamari Star Cruiser (set 7754), where she discusses the latest Rebel plans to defeat the Empire once and for all.

DATA FILE
SET: 7754 *Home One* Mon Calamari Star Cruiser
YEAR: 2009
PIECES: 5
EQUIPMENT: Cape
VARIANTS: 1

Unique torso printed with silver Chandrilian Freedom Medal

Same head piece as Princess Leia, another former senator

Tousled hair
Mon Mothma's tousled reddish-brown hair is the same piece as that used for the Clone Wars version of Anakin Skywalker's minifigure.

Mon Mothma is the only minifigure to wear a white cape in LEGO *Star Wars*

Mon Mothma
REBEL COMMANDER

27

Admirable Admiral Ackbar commands the Rebel assault on the second Death Star from his flagship *Home One* (set 7754). Ackbar appears only in this one LEGO set— but his minifigure plays a pivotal part in LEGO *Star Wars* history! Ackbar is one of three Mon Calamari minifigures, but his unique commander uniform makes him stand out.

Home One Mon Calamari Star Cruiser (set 7754)
Admiral Ackbar coordinates the Rebel assault on the second Death Star in this set. He has a swiveling and sliding command chair, and a tactical computer that can mount his lap. The set even contains his coffee cup!

Admiral Ackbar
REBEL SUPREME COMMANDER

Solid plastic Mon Calamari head with large, bulbous eyes. The Mon Calamari officer and Nahdar Vebb have the same head piece

Metallic command insignia denotes Ackbar's high rank

Unique LEGO torso features a cream Mon Calamari naval jerkin over a white space suit

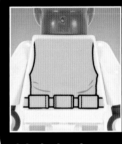

Admiral attire
The details of Ackbar's jerkin and utility belt continue on the back of his torso piece. Ackbar keeps vital command equipment in the six pockets of his belt.

Reddish-brown webbed hands

Special set
Admiral Ackbar also appears in the exclusive LEGO *Star Wars* Collectible Display Set 2, which was available for one day only at the 2009 San Diego Comic-Con. Crix Madine (opposite) and Jedi Knight Luke Skywalker were also included in the set.

DATA FILE
SET: 7754 *Home One* Mon Calamari Star Cruiser
YEAR: 2009
PIECES: 3
EQUIPMENT: None
VARIANTS: 1

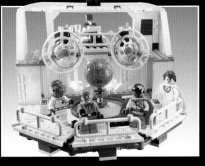

***Home One* Mon Calamari Star Cruiser (set 7754)**
Together with other Rebel leaders Mon Mothma, Admiral Ackbar, and Lando Calrissian, General Crix Madine plans the destruction of the second Death Star during the Battle of Endor.

General Crix Madine has not always been loyal to the Rebel cause—he was once an Imperial Army officer—but he is now an important leader of the Rebel Alliance with invaluable insider knowledge. His minifigure is exclusive to just one limited edition LEGO set, but he is there when it counts—the most crucial battle in the LEGO *Star Wars* galaxy!

Hair first
General Crix Madine was the first LEGO minifigure to sport the standard short hair piece in a dark tan color. It has since been seen on only one other minifigure: a faceless mannequin in a shop in the LEGO City theme.

General Crix Madine's happy, brown-bearded face is unique to his minifigure

Collar pips denote rank

Black-gloved hands

Communications badge allows Madine to contact Rebel command and other leaders

This tan torso piece was created specifically for Madine's minifigure

General Crix Madine
REBEL LEADER

DATA FILE

SET: 7754 *Home One* Mon Calamari Star Cruiser
YEAR: 2009
PIECES: 4
EQUIPMENT: None
VARIANTS: 1

Penguin Random House

Editors Hannah Dolan, Shari Last,
Victoria Taylor, and Matt Jones
Designers Anne Sharples and Jon Hall
Senior Producer Lloyd Robertson
Senior DTP Designer David McDonald
Managing Editor Simon Hugo
Design Manager Guy Harvey
Creative Manager Sarah Harland
Art Director Lisa Lanzarini
Publisher Julie Ferris
Publishing Director Simon Beecroft

Additional minifigures photographed by Huw Millington,
Ace Kim, Jeremy Beckett, and Tony Wood

First published in the United States in 2015
by DK Publishing
345 Hudson Street, New York, New York 10014

Contains material previously published in
LEGO® Star Wars® Character Encyclopedia (2011)

001-284485-Feb/15

Page design copyright ©2015 Dorling Kindersley Limited
A Penguin Random House Company

A catalog record for this book is available from
the Library of Congress.

ISBN: 978-5-0010-1296-2

Color reproduction by Media Development Printing Ltd, UK
Printed and bound in China

Dorling Kindersley would like to thank:
Jonathan W. Rinzler, Troy Alders, Rayne Roberts, Pablo
Hidalgo, and Leland Chee at Lucasfilm; Stephanie
Lawrence, Randi Sørensen, Lisbeth Langjkær, Jens
Kronvold Frederiksen, Chris Bonven Johansen, and John
McCormack at the LEGO Group; LEGO Star Wars
collectors Ace Kim and Huw Millington; Emma Grange,
Lisa Stock, Sarah Harland, Ellie Hallsworth, and Nicola
Brown for editorial support; and Owen Bennett for
design support on the cover.

www.dk.com
www.LEGO.com
www.starwars.com

A WORLD OF IDEAS:
SEE ALL THERE IS TO KNOW